Breathing the West: Great Basin Poems by Liane Ellison Norman is a rendering of inheritance, an historical document that speaks the journals of the writer's father, Western range ecologist Lincoln Ellison. In poems often interwoven with actual journal excerpts, Norman pays tribute to the life and work of a man of passion and commitment to the environment, especially to the area of the Wasatch Plateau region of Utah. These poems breathe the West—the love of the land, the hard prices paid in blood, water, and soil—but also they breathe the spirit of a man who gave a way of seeing to a young girl; this seeing now alive with adventure, love, and family in these beautifully crafted poems.

—Jan Beatty, author of *Red Sugar*

Other Books by Liane Ellison Norman

Hammer of Justice: Molly Rush and the Plowshares Eight
(PPI Books 1998).

Stitches in Air: A Novel About Mozart's Mother
(Smoke & Mirrors Press, 2001).

The Duration of Grief
(Smoke & Mirrors Press, 2005).

Keep: Poems by Liane Ellison Norman/ Art by Ruey Brodine Morelli
(Smoke & Mirrors Press, 2009).

Mere Citizens: United, Civil, Disobedient
(Smoke & Mirrors Press, 2011).

Driving Near the Old Federal Arsenal: Poetry
(Finishing Line Press, 2012)

Breathing the West

Great Basin Poems

Liane Ellison Norman

Working Lives Series
Bottom Dog Press
Huron, Ohio

Credits:

Editor: Laura Smith

Photos by Lincoln Ellison and Liane Ellison Norman

Acknowledgements

A number of these poems have been published in a chapbook, *Roundtrip*, by Yesterday's Parties Press, 2012.
Others appeared in the following publications:
"Pruning Roses in March," Pittsburgh *City Paper*;
"Inheritance," Practical Men" and "Mother Sewing," *Kestrel*;
"The Great Basin" and "Tectonics," *The Fourth River*;
"A Mountain Falls on Route 65," *Pittsburgh Post Gazette*;
"Washing," *Voices From the Attic*;
"Taking," *The New People*, newsletter of the Thomas Merton Center;
"Memory of Stars," *5 A.M.*;
"Roundtrip," *Platte Valley Review*.

These poems celebrate the good fortune and lasting influence of a childhood in the Wasatch Mountains of south-central Utah. I was lucky in my parents—Lincoln Ellison, a range ecologist who worked nearly all his short life for the Forest Service; and Laurel Elver Ellison, an elementary school teacher with a strong sense of civic responsibility. My three younger sisters, Laurel Ellison, Linda Jessup and Linnea Brecunier, were my childhood playmates and are now my friends. I am also lucky in my adult family: my endlessly generous husband, Robert Norman, and both interesting and beloved offspring, Andy Norman, Marie Norman, the late Emily Norman Davidson, their partners, Heidi Norman and Matt Weiss, and children, Katie Davidson, Reece and Kai Norman, Maya and Dev Weiss, all of whom have made my life rich and interesting.

Particular thanks for this volume of poems go to the wizardry of poet and friend Jan Beatty and the Madwomen in the Attic, particularly those in the manuscript class of 2008—Tess Barry, Lois Greenberg, Marilyn Marsh Noll, Susan Sailer, Amy Sutton, Ann Tomer, Bernadette Ulsamer, Lori Wilson and the late Christina Murdock. Madwomen are a large and generous tribe. Todd Sanders is endlessly helpful with fonts, formatting, and habits computers have. Thanks also to Laura and Larry Smith of Bottom Dog Press for being good to work with.

Table of Contents

I

No branch stirred, no bird fluttered or uttered a sound.
A white stillness, diffused light from the gray clouds
and white snow, which perhaps is what Death is like.

—Lincoln Ellison, 1930

Liane, Linnea, Mother, Linda, and Laurel before Alpine Cabin

Grand Opera at 8,850 Feet

for Nathalie Hansen

We named him Billy Deer, fed him with a baby bottle.
When they took him to the game preserve

Mama Dell said he followed her along the fence,
tears running down his face and we believed her.

We made villages of mud and moss for fairies. Took
our little sisters to the Froggy Pond. Held the pulsing

emerald frogs basketed in hands, let them skip back
under water. We played hide-and-seek as night fell,

ran outside in rainstorms in our underpants.
We terrified the little kids, waving her mother's headless

dress form in the window. We made up plays for everyone,
she and I the principals, little sisters supernumeraries.

We warbled like singers on the Saturday Metropolitan
Opera broadcasts, tales of Pythagoras and Penelope,

up to our eyebrows in dastardly deeds, painted
our imaginary fingernails with blood.

The scenery was larkspur, beautiful and poisonous.
We made the plot up as we went.

Rain Shadow

Pacific moisture blows from west
to east, precipitates, watering
western slopes. Dried out winds
flow up and over and into the desert.

These ancient mountains float
on magma. Sierras pull away
from Rockies, stretching
the Great Basin. Someday it may

break apart. Then arid mountainsides
will harvest ocean's moisture,
Wasatch Range casting its rain shadow east,
west coast an archipelago, out to sea.

Fathom

Birds of Cornwall blown off course,
taking a migration break
on this almost-island,
warmed by the Gulf Stream-—
storks, falcons, gulls—
soaring above the ocean,
wading on rocky shores.

A fathom forward by a fathom vertical,
Cornish miners said
about the space
they worked in.

A fathom is the length
of outstretched arms,
a six-foot wingspan.

Aunt Connie sent a picture postcard,
Man engine in Dolcoath Mine,
Camborne, Redruth, Cornwall, 1892,
open-sided elevator
down 234 fathoms
invented by the miners, who also
invented the surface steam engine
to lower and lift them so they could
pry out copper and tin. Invented
miner's lamp and steam pump.

Connie wrote how her grandfather—
ten years old—just fit the 18-inch space.
Man engine took him down to a day's work.
She wrote, *Those men of the underground*
greatly revered now.

I try to fathom a boy working below the Atlantic,
where kids like him drowned
with their fathers, brothers,
or lost an eye, a face, to explosion.
Filled the graveyards
fathom deep with miners.

Knitting Needle

In memory of my grandmother, Alrena Beatrice Thomas Ellison

A.O. walked out. Alrena and the children lived
in the chicken house, sold eggs and fruit. She baked

Cornish pasties. The children sold them from the wagon
they collected laundry in and took back washed and ironed.

She sold corsets, Avon products door-to-door. At the birth
of each grandchild, put $100 in a bank account, gave us

a set of *Encyclopedia Britannica*. For high school graduation
sent us each a Webster's *Dictionary*. She mended, darned,

crocheted a lacy shawl for me, braided a thick wool rug
from our outgrown winter coats. Said she'd performed

abortions on herself with a knitting needle. No details.
By then she must have known her husband feckless,

but how did she know to guide the long, thin steel up
out of sight inside her blood-drenched folds?

First Journals

Man of the house at fifteen when his father
walked out, Lincoln worked in the garden,
pruned fruit trees, berry canes, cleaned

the garage, kept two jalopies running,
tended a nearby farmer's smudge pots.
Recorded what he saw—spiders, owl scat—

a life-long habit: the natural world could not
abandon him. Later, loss of soil was tragedy:
like warfare, it threatened civilization.

Reading his journals was like
the grown-up conversations we had
walking home from the library

where I worked for money to go to college.
Don't worry about grades, he said. *Just learn*.

Bogalusa Romance, 1932

from Lincoln Ellison's letters to Laurel Elver

I am beginning, Lincoln wrote his beloved,
to take an aboriginal delight in nudity.

Walking back to his room from plots
where he made measurements
of broad leaf pine, he stopped to swim
as often as he could. *Ah, the luxury*
of the cool water! What strange, bell-like
chimings it makes to the submerged ear,
and how I love to see it pour, swift-swirling,
around my higher shoulder!

Lincoln wrote to Laurel, *if a bumblebee*
is drunk, is he to blame or the flower? Would
the rising cost of postage—the 3¢ stamp—
make writing to her a luxury? *Sweetheart,*
you've been a luxury since ever I've known you.

Finding Vega in the night sky linked them,
the brightest star of Lyra, burning itself up
faster than the rival sun. Laurel sent her kiss
by way of Vega, occasioning a lesson
in astronomy. *If your kiss should travel*
with the speed of light, it would drop
down to me in my 84th year.

Bravado

Lanky and lonely,
Lincoln was young
and full of beans,
thought his boss
a mere timeserver.
Before he left
Louisiana's heat and bugs,
he filed a report
that said so
to the Bogalusa office
of the Forest Service.

His boss scolded.
Lincoln should have
showed it to *him* first.
He'd have corrected
misimpressions.

Lincoln wrote
to his beloved,
I stood there,
round-eyed,
with a face that
(I imagined)
was one
of seraphic innocence,
tho there was
a satanical grin
bubbling around
in back of the mask.
Just what
I had hoped for!
Hot Diggity!
It might get me
into trouble yet!

Waiting

Young and poor, Lincoln wrote in his journal:
that by 1933, when he'd be 25, he expected
he'd have gone on *at least two scientific expeditions*
to foreign countries, be recognized as a leader of my field.
Not until then, he wrote, *is it time to talk of getting married.*

But in 1933 the Great Depression altered everything.
Refugees from prairie states—land denuded of soil by wind,
destructive farming practices—headed south and west.
Jobs were scarce. In Europe the Reichstag Fire, first
concentration camp. Nothing was as he expected.

Nevertheless, Lincoln asked Laurel to marry him.
Next day, an offer of work in Idaho, Priest River Station:
report immediately. They married in a hurry
under a rose-trimmed arch on a dewy evening,
the bride in a skin of ruffled satin.

The two virgins had just one night together.
He caught the train next morning
for Spokane, Missoula, Priest River,
wrote her, he knew *genuine content*
for the first time in his life.

Then news that he might have to supervise
a crew of CCC or ECW men in the wilds.
April ended, May, then June. Sometimes
Forest Service money ran out. Plans changed,
changed again, but he always had work.

Back in her little town, Laurel wrote,
everyone looked askance, wondered why
her bridegroom had done a bunk.

They waited through July, through August.
The Forest Service, he wrote, *is not going to keep us*
apart. He had saved up money: *Why not put in the winter*

in the northwoods? $200 will grubstake a pretty long winter.
There would be time for reading & writing, many a ski
and snowshoe journey, many a long evening of talk
and love-making and music—Hai ya!

Laurel was packed, ready to join him.
Then, once again the Forest Service was out of money.
He'd work for the Park Service in Glacier Park,
mapping timber types. Women not allowed.

He wrote, *Come, Dear, let us find Vega every nite,*
each of us: it will be our own particular kind of prayer.

Snow fell in September. In November, finally,
the letters stop. They're what I have to go on.

They'd been married seven months before they,
who would in five years be my parents,
first lived together.

Nearby the Graves

On the prairie swept by wind
Mother's blue-baby sister died.

Her father built a tiny coffin.
Her mother lined it with pretty

fabric, buried the baby in the field.
My father's journal says they found

the homestead in Roscoe, Colorado
as they drove back west—

Washington DC to Missoula, Montana.
They knocked on the farmer's door,

who showed them the little grave
he'd carefully plowed around

all those years, asked if he could move it
to nearby the graves of his children.

Great Basin Experiment Station, 1938

Glimpsed a *twinkling butterfly with a slash of white across
dark wings*, Lincoln wrote Laurel and the baby, visiting
her parents,. At 30 he was Director of the Great Basin
Experiment Station, fifteen miles above the little town

of Ephraim, Utah, streets wide enough for covered wagons
four abreast. For the first time he drove up the hairpin road
past sagebrush, Major's Flat, over the first cattle-guard
into the Manti-LaSalle National Forest, past Power Ditch,

spangled with wild roses, tin can on a stick for overheated
radiators. Around a bend startled by white trunks
of quaking aspen against dark fir and spruce. Gateway
of whitewashed logs, silent welcome to the Station. Or

maybe he went on up, past Frog Pond, over Bluebell Bridge,
past Philly Flat to Alpine and the snow-surveyor's cabin,
snowdrifts nibbled at the edges by dog-tooth violets.
Or further up to Skyline Drive's immensity of quiet.

Back down at the Station, he imagined Laurel—*her delight
when she first goes thru* the West House, the ground behind
carpeted with yellow violets. The West House anchored
white buildings with green shutters set around an oval—

flagpole, fountain, wild hollyhocks, wild roses, many-flowered
sunflowers—a lodge for visitors, office, barn, garage
and workshop. *Oh,* he wrote to Laurel, how he longed
for their earlier days in the hot sun with the creak

of packsack leather, alone, the two of them, *amongst huge
mountains, over a little fire, and dropping off to sleep
'with the starlight on our faces.'* When he first arrived,
sorted through old records in the silent office, he was

alarmed: *technics here are in a parlous state.* At first
it was learning about the place it would be his to run.
But his research and writing became what one historian
has called *the most comprehensive vegetational history
of the Wasatch Plateau, before or since.*

Philadelphia Flat

Mother sent me with lunch in a paper bag down from the Alpine Cabin,
across the icy stream, through timothy grass, aster and yarrow,
across the hairpin road and up the opposite slope to Philadelphia Flat.

It was only a mile, but at six a journey of difficulty and peril.
My father was charting vegetal growth in quadrats,
plots fenced against browsing deer and elk. I cut sideways

among dense currant bushes hung with fruit just short of garnet,
threaded among granite boulders, couldn't see where I was headed—
lost. The sky so wide, so high, a burning blue. My heart choked me.

Suddenly a winding corridor, rock wall to the right, hill to the left,
circles of tough grass where fairies danced at night. A weasel, winter white,
poised upright on a gnarl of wind-blown root, stared at me, I stared at him,

a long, enchanted moment. Then he was gone like smoke. I scrambled up
to picnic with my father, couldn't find a way to tell him how
that wizard weasel, his magical passageway, had rescued me.

When I Was Seven

the war in Europe moved in on the domed
wooden radio with its gothic front where
Let's Pretend arrived every Saturday, brought
to us by Uncle Bill and Cream O' Wheat.

Nathalie and I conspired to send a bomb
to Hitler hidden in a bouquet of wild flowers,
or better, in a jar of mayonnaise: either bomb
or mayo would kill him. I built cities

out of dominoes where Hitler lived
and bombed them flat with other dominoes,
but he hid under the couch and I fled onto it
so he couldn't grab me by the ankles.

Canning

In late summer, we all labored, Mother
aproned and sweating, face red, hair curling,
over the wood stove, boiling jars and lids,

syrup that magnified Queen Anne cherries,
apricots, apples, all from our own trees. Quart
jars stood on the kitchen counter till the lids

popped, signaling a seal, safe to store against
winter. They lined the basement pantry,
gold and rubies of Aladdin's cave.

Miss Hardy

They said she held the school tough
down the stairwell by his hair, dropped
him for his insolence. Flipped Jimmy
Wolfe over my head when he lined up
on the wrong side. Conducted the band
behind the classroom piano I played,
spitting punctuation my direction.

Elementary school music teacher, tall
and strong as a bony man, pop-eyes,
swept-back copper curls like Chore Boy
scrubbing pads. Wore three dresses,
each in turn, old lady lace-up shoes.

Fitted a fist into her open mouth,
Way down upon the Swan—ee Riv—ah;
told us stories of the operas to be broadcast
the next day, batting invisible eyelashes
as shy Madama Butterfly, dying Mimi.
I listened to all the operas on the radio,
wooden cathedral of that sounding love.

Ecology of Sisters

For just a moment, my father confused
umbilicus with penis, rejoiced to have
a son. *Bossy big sister*, says the second,

who learned dependence as the way
to get along, then adventured from an airless
marriage. The third, insatiable to prove

herself against two bigger sisters, grew
strenuous in her accomplishment.
The fourth, much younger, learned to launch

herself and land as lightly as a cat, all nine lives
intact. Sturdy as pioneer women, we
have opinions—*Take a breath and lose your turn*,

one husband says. We're tuned to the same pitch
of genes, tribal voice and gesture. We see each other
seldom, but always with affection and ferocity.

Mother Sewing

She made clothes for our Christmas Madame Alexander
dolls, mine blond like me, my dark-haired sister's dark.
Wool coats from scraps of her winter coat lined
with matching rayon; for shoes, the finger tips

of her worn gloves. All made in secret, though we heard
the hum of her sewing machine, refused to put two
and two together: we had little sisters to fool
and wanted to believe in Santa Claus. Before I went

to college—had to take a formal—we found a gleaming
yardage of green and pale gray shimmering stuff, the bodice
lined with silvery silk, green velvet straps, conferring royal
carriage. Maybe it was Butterick, maybe Vogue,

patterns she'd taught me to lay on the straight of cloth,
some pieces on the bias, stitching on the Singer she'd bought
(and my father groused about—*a luxury.*) She made us
pinafores, sunbonnets, curtains, upholstery for the couch

and chairs my father refinished. I pushed her away
in adolescence—she tried to land on moons that circled
my private planet. I wanted physics; she insisted on Pep Club
so I'd be popular. She wanted a pretty, pliant daughter:

I was plain and academic. I fought her and she fought back;
each wounded the other. But she stood by me, called it *crucifixion*
when the men I worked with savaged my accomplishment
in secret so I had no way of answering. She taught me always

to baste the zippers in, the darts, collars, sleeves,
taught me to save the scraps.

Tectonics

A geologist told me we're headed for extinction.
I grieve for my grandchildren's children's children,
Pergolesi, George Eliot, soft organisms with brief
lives. The tiny trilobite I held, black jewel

in my palm, perfect spine, antennae, 300 million
years old, found in mountains once under seas,
while continents broke apart, collided.
Native Americans called them *little water bugs*

in big rocks. My father wrote of the *unstable,*
molten sea our solid earth is floating on, a giant
under everything, turning in sleep, hip up, shoulder
over, knocking up mountains, making waves.

On the Wasatch Plateau, above timber, the fish that once
swam in Lake Bonneville still brush against my face.

Alibi

*It is easier to imagine a desert to have been a desert
since Creation day than to imagine that it may be a desert
because of man. It is easier when floods come down
from the mountains, to assume floods an inevitable part
of man's lot since the days of Noah....Surely such vast
consequences of such remote and awful origin, cannot
be the fault of man—they must be acts of God!*

—Lincoln Ellison, 1941

Not us, they said, since how else would they earn
their daily bread, govern as Mormon churchmen?

Stockmen wanted to graze their herds atop steep
mountainsides as their fathers had done for free

forever on the Wasatch Plateau. They held for God.
If they, mere men, who owned or ran the herds,

denuding slopes of plants that held the soil where it
ran off in mud-rock floods, fouling towns below,

were culpable.... How else would herders, Jensens,
Christensens, Scandinavian converts, thrive? *Not us*,

we say, who pump and dig the ancient bones
of insects, ferns, ancestral trees. *Not us*, we say

who sell and burn and loose the gases to the sky.
No one's responsible. The toddler, when she broke

a vase, said her imaginary horse,
Big Jumper, did it.

II

When lovers quarrel, mark you this:
all is not settled in the kiss —
one may take and one may give,
when one is water in a sieve;
both may give and neither take,
as mingle waters in a lake;
but if both take, then God forfend!
What once was love is at an end.

—Lincoln Ellison

Lincoln Ellison playing guitar in the Alpine Cabin

We'd come from Cornwall

where my ancestors lie buried,
to the mouth of the Dart in Devon,
through quiet, green fields
down roads so narrow
we could hear the scrape
of hedgerow against bus.

Bells of ancient churches—
St. Clement, St. Petrox, St. Savior—
rang a clangor we felt on our skins,
a din that silenced the birds.

We searched for my husband's
Dartmouth forebears, wandered
in graveyards, scoured records
in the bright new library's microfiche,
found tales of wars—Norse raiders,
Crusaders, Norman invasion,
the invasion of Utah Beach.

And found we're related
by Prayer Book Rebellion,
when holdouts from Devon and Cornwall
refused the English king's allegiance
to himself, fifty-five hundred
crushed to blood and broken bone.

But now the waterfront sparkles—
whitecaps, sailboats,
gulls, swans, fish and chips.

Cemetery

After dinner Lincoln took a walk with his slender wife,
plump sister, through the cemetery of tiny Ashland, Montana,

bounded by Rosebud and Tongue rivers. He noted
the tended, ungrazed grass around gravestones compared

to land over-grazed and trampled on high ranges. Here,
land protected for the dead; there, a commodity, a living

that put the living at risk. He searched for primitive places,
baseline for comparison, found Elk Knoll just off the top

of Skyline Drive, an out-of-the-way pocket of land
without nearby water to draw livestock, protected

for fifty years. Now a boulder with his name and dates
on a brass plaque marks a Research Natural Area.

The newest threat is ATVs and ORVs
that rip up vegetation, soil and silence.

The Great Basin

The Pacific plate shoved the California coast
up and east. Rock crumpled like fabric in a fist
making Sierra and Wasatch ranges and the basin

between. When glaciers melted the basin filled.
Lake Bonneville spread over Utah, Nevada, into
Idaho until it overflowed through Red Rock Pass,

swarming with watery life, recorded as fossils on high-up
slopes. Still a work in progress—mountains in motion,
tectonic forces pulling Sierras away from the Wasatch—

these tipped and folded mountains, terraced by receding
water, deltas where streams ran out, depositing
rich soil in alluvial fans with mammoth bones,

bones of musk ox who had come to drink and sank
in marshy swamps. A lava cave housed a camel's
skull, scrap from some carnivore's lunch.

August 6, 1945

A week after Pearl Harbor my father
wrote in his journal that as he did
the breakfast dishes he got to thinking
about the war *to such an extent that I wept.*

He was exempt, his work considered
crucial to the home-front, but he hated
the effluvium of propaganda, collapse
of sympathy for difference, diversion
of resources. When the war ended

I was eight. We drove to my grandfather's
church, I on my knees looking out the back
car window, seeing black tar patches bloom
in the pavement like explosions. They had dropped
A-bombs on people like me, my newborn sister.

Germination

Lincoln found *germination*
where no one else thot it would be—
in shady spots, just free of snow,
which <u>ought</u> to be too cold.

Years later, digging down
nine feet through snow,
he found a world beyond
what he'd thought to see—

green- and yellow-leaved plants
being grazed by gophers
all winter long—
illumination in cold dark.

Practical Men

Stayed home and dug post holes today.

—Lincoln Ellison at 17

Scholar and dreamer, Lincoln liked practical men,
the Norwegian sheepherder in outback Montana
who showed him how to castrate sheep with his teeth.

He weeded the Victory Garden, fixed the office typewriter
so all but the carriage return worked, built shower houses,
decks and walls for tents, bought giant cooking pots

for the 1939 seminar on range management. He built
three rooms on the second floor of our house, grew
a buccaneer's mustache, chortled as he twirled the ends.

On Sundays he made pancakes, flipping them up,
catching with the frying pan. Trying to figure out
original growth in the sub-alpine zone of the Wasatch Plateau,

he read back issues of *The Ephraim Enterprise*, talked to
old-timers. A 74-year-old sheepherder, remembered
the range covered in broadleaf plants, not grasses,

though another spoke up for grasses so tall
they nearly hid the sheep and cattle run by herders
for their owners over the range they thought was free.

Lincoln said, human beings are *never so clearly an element
in the balance of nature as when they destroy the balance.*

Alpine Cabin

Each late June, the road then almost clear of snowdrifts, we arrived,
Mother's head aching from altitude. But she'd spread out the tablecloth,
hang the blue-plaid ruffles she'd made across each window, send us
out for wildflowers—home-making bouquet—while Daddy started
the fire with aspen kindling, adding coal from the dented scuttle.

Some mornings at first light I'd wake to see an elk lofting his rack
of antlers, nosing the air for danger. I'd watch as long as my bladder
held, then dash the city block across the buttercup-bordered stream,
to the outhouse. Sometimes the elk stood still, watching this wild thing,
bareheaded, scramble on two legs. Sometimes he'd startle, bound away.

The cabin was square, log-and-block, built for snow surveyors,
icy water in the sink. The stream outside cooled milk, fresh melons
brought up from Ephraim once a week with books from the library.
I went back twenty years ago, remembrance bubbling like the spring
that fed the stream—my mother's flowered tablecloth faded,

blue ruffles grey, drooping along the tops of windows. Hanging
on the wall, the galvanized tub where we girls bathed in water
heated on the coal stove, taking turns. Always coffee in the black
enamel pot, perfume of bread rising or fresh baked. Just off
the kitchen, a pantry, space for cans of Spam, Borden's

canned milk, quart jars of last summer's tomatoes, peaches,
apricots, battered table where Daddy worked on his *Subalpine Vegetation
of the Wasatch Plateau*. Six cots in the only other room, each flanked
by an orange crate holding crayons for the good sides of used paper,
scissors, tape. On clear nights, we had a bonfire, sparks jostling stars.

Daddy played his guitar and Mother taught us songs.
Nights inside, by kerosene lamplight I made into paper dolls,
all the characters in books—Glinda the Good Witch, Alice, Red Queen,
Rapunzel. As the kitchen fire burned down, we were quick into cold
cocoons of canvas, kapock, Army surplus khaki wool.

On Top

The rule was to stay put for fear of getting lost. We'd
driven out rocky Skyline Drive—*on top*, we called it,
above timber—in the Forest Service truck. I'd brought

Alice in Wonderland, read and re-read till I knew it by heart.
Daddy left me with the hostage lunch in needlegrass, foxtail,
timothy, meadowlark-embroidered air, Indian paintbrush

burning like tiny fires, drove off to check some quadrats.
I read the strange adventures of the girl of sudden height
and shrink. Sun spangled the grass taller than I was,

slipping down a rabbit hole to sleep. Alight in golden
grasses, I woke, Daddy nowhere in sight. Below me
stands of fir and spruce, the sky such pulsing blue it hurt

to look, and in the valley pastel quilted farms.
The only sound, the tick and scuttle of small creatures.
Should I go look for him? The hillside, trackless, dazzled.

A red tailed hawk circling below, slight featherings
to sail on drafts of air, kept me from crying out.
Then, there he was, neither of us lost.

Cleaning House Before Moving

Every drawer—dark insides that collect
hair, paper clips, bobby pins, rubber bands,
where you keep things that may some day
be useful but rarely are—swept, tipped out
and scrubbed, windows washed, ashes raked,
kindling box filled, extra matches left.

Mother said to leave the house as we
would like to find it. She swept, mopped
the floors, backing out the front door,
rinsed the mop under the tap in back,
wrung out and left to dry beside the door,
edged by yellow violets in spring.

Treasure

Ogden, Utah 1945

Cranky from the crowded drive, quarreling
in the backseat of the '39 Chevy, the baby
on Mother's lap—our first house at dusk.

Mother had found, settled on it herself,
a big white house, lofty sycamore in front.
We raced through immaculate rooms,

echoing walls, linoleum, the cold wood stove.
My sisters would sleep upstairs, mine the room
off the screened back porch. I pulled open

the drawer of the left-behind, painted-white
dresser to find presents—outgrown toys
the Olsons had left for each of us. Mine,

a leather sack with a ball and jacks, brilliant
color worn to the intersections. Ballerinas—
Sylvia, ruby-rose, Estella, peacock-green,—

twirled on their points. Unless I was tossing
the ball, scooping, catching. My father and I
sanded, scraped, found a marble top, burled

panels on the drawers. Best of all, square nails,
hand forged, still hold my dresser together.

Plenitude

Under my pillow, reward for my first lost tooth,
a tiny string of silver figures, joined hand and foot,
cut with fingernail scissors from the wrapper of a stick
of chewing gum, a gift from fairies, who later brought
a gauzy handkerchief with scalloped gilded edges,

a small ceramic kewpie doll, both made in Occupied Japan.
That first tooth fell out just after the war, but we'd kept
a cow, had cream and butter, a pig for sausages and soap.
War-rationed gas and sugar didn't matter much
in Ephraim where everyone could walk and honey

was to hand. When a cedar waxwing chick fell from its nest,
I mothered him, fed him chopped egg on the fat end
of a toothpick and he grew tame enough to ride my shoulder
to school until a flock of waxwings in late autumn sky
reminded him he was a bird. What I lusted for

was a *store boughten* dress made of caramel corduroy
in Christensen's General Store. Mother said we couldn't
afford it. But I got to act Snow White in the first grade play.
The prince, his nose a snotty slick, woke me with a kiss.
A quarter century later, after college, marriage, three years

in Asia, three children, I went back and greeted Dewey
Anderson at the gas station. In minutes everyone
knew Linc and Laurel's daughter was in town: Dewey
fixed our flat tire; the drug store cashed our check;
we heard how Daddy had hiked up the moonlit mountain,

moleskin climbers on his skis on Christmas Eve,
to get the tree lights left behind in the basement
of our Station house, skied back down the glittering
mountain, arriving just in time for Santa Claus
to come and go, leaving homemade plenty.

Rules

You can tell a lady by her cuticles,
Mother, the preacher's daughter, said,
and whether she crosses her legs at the ankles.

Her mother, the preacher's wife, decreed
a piano's *legs* were *limbs,* a bull was a *gentleman cow,*
and I should not sew marionette costumes

on the Sabbath. Shoes should never be down
at heel nor seams of stockings crooked. Never
wear blue with green nor red with pink.

No plaid with stripes nor silver with gold.
White shoes between Easter and Labor Day,
neither before nor after. Above all, *never, never,
never let a boy know how smart you are.*

Wilson R. Thornley

That flame of hair
rimming his head,
cocked like a bird's,
smile of sheer delight,
wizard with invisible
powers. Taught
in a high school class-
room at the end
of a hall with marble
floors and walls
to write with sensory
detail, verve and clarity
to fit voice and breath.

He died long years ago
but came to my dream,
answered the fear
that I had done too
little to change the world,

tipped his head, said
You never know
what it is you change.

An Old Woman of Uncertain Memory

Her mind had begun its long, slow ravel and misconnect when she told
      my sisters
how she'd lived in one small shack after another in fierce prairie wind;
how her father, Methodist faith-healer, homesteaded;
how he'd been disowned by his German Lutheran parents in Wisconsin;
how he'd met her mother in Iowa;
how she'd pounded on Colorado rocks with sticks when she went out
      to play;
how she scared the lurking rattlesnakes away.

Home Economics

The boys took wood or metal shop;
      girls, home ec, cooking and sewing.
           Not fair: I wanted to work with tools

that made ear-splitting noise, come home
      with book shelves or fix motors.
           Now I'm glad I learned more

about sewing, easier with a teacher
      than with Mother, learning to make
           bound buttonholes,

how to measure hems taking into account
      legs of slightly different lengths,
           how to set collars in and sleeves,

basting everything. Our big night was a fashion show.
      I wore the yellow organdy I'd made
           with clean, low neck,

my first high heels and later, when the gush
      of menstrual blood did not know
           how to stop, thought I'd die,

bleeding all over that
      petaled daffodil skirt
           and into the torturing shoes.

The Mountain Groans

Pocket gophers displaced five tons of dirt
in an 80 acre plot. Lincoln wrote in 1946

that when the land was already overgrazed,
gopher digging loosened soil to wash away.

In 2007 on the eastern side of the Wasatch Plateau
the Crandall Canyon Coal Mine collapsed.

They'd dug out bituminous coal, leaving
bituminous pillars, then dug the pillars out.

Six miners and three rescuers were killed.
Scientists said the cave-in made seismic needles

jump. The owner said earthquakes were to blame.
Miners said that underground they could hear

the mountain groan.

The Scholastic Aptitude Test, 1955

Who wanted, on that frozen day, to go to college, anyway?
There were only six of us scheduled to take the test in January
and so the only school to give it was in Salt Lake, a high school
left unheated during Christmas break. I drove there from Ogden
and burned through the morning, language aptitude, stored body heat.

By afternoon the content part: *Who was Sun Yat Sen?* I was too
cold by then to care, remembered Jack London's "To Build a Fire,"
hands too stiff to light the last few matches, the dog he might
kill to use the carcass for warmth too skittish, feet too numb to walk,
hoping his friends would find him in unlikely time to save his life.

The icy air outside seemed warm, the drive, a thawing
back to life. When I got home—to the forgiving place
I knew by smell and feel, where I could find my way
in the dark—I found a new green sweater on my bed,
a gift from Mother, who knew it had mattered.

Breathing the West

First gasps, provisional. Missoula
winter air. I filled my lungs high

in the Wasatch Mountains. Learned
mountain weathers above timber,

tingle of aspen leaves. Then left
for Grinnell, Boston, Kathmandu,

Pittsburgh. Hardly noticed how it was
to breathe those different airs.

But when I went back one summer
to Snow Basin, knew, *my DNA's from here.*

The back slopes of Mt. Ogden, the air
that taught me how to breathe.

III

I seem to revolve around a central idea
like a planet around the sun,
and every once in a while I am turned
to catch a glimpse of it.

—Lincoln Ellison

Great Basis Experiment Station, 1939; lodge, office, East House back right

Short Stories of Short Lives

Camborne Graveyard, Cornwall 2005

Once center of the earth for tin and copper, mines
found with dowsing rods, finally exhausted.

Rocky appendix of land, washed by Atlantic
waters and the English Channel, joined to

and divided from Devon by the River Tamar.
Wild moors, pastures late-summer emerald,

sea birds screaming, small birds gossiping
in gorse and heather stillness. Wesley Chapel's

graveyard full of weathered wafers, sinking
stones, my great great grandparents. Short

stories of short lives lost in mines, in childbed,
migrations to places where ores, still plentiful,

drew hardy immigrants. How did they pull up
roots that ran so deep in familiar soil, hazard

hostile oceans, join the far-off Gold Rush,
put already tired backs into foreign mines?

Camborne's quiet weave of birdsong, declining
curve of street bordered by gray stone houses

with lace curtains. Abandoned brick chimneys
of worked-out mines still stand in fields.

Tall Tales in Utah

Mama Dell told the tale—
with utter conviction—
of a man whose neck
was caught in the spokes
of a wagon wheel, which ran
another fifteen miles.
Paul Hansen drawled,
Was he dead?

*

Traveling by car, looking
up at steep hillsides, we got
the geologic history: ancient
lakes, sedimentation, volcanic
thrust and fold, and Daddy
explained how Wasatch cows
were bred with shorter uphill,
longer downhill legs.
Herders had to get it right,
uphill legs uphill, downhill
legs down, or the cows
would fall right off the slope.

*

When sheep got going across
the road, they seethed around
the car and there was no getting
through until they'd all followed
the leader, a thick boil of bleats.
Count them, Daddy told us,
Count the legs and divide by four.

Snow in 1939

The photo shows the Station buried deeper
than eaves, spruce tops laden like saplings.
Ski tracks run from the roof of the Lodge
toward West and South houses and toward me,
a smooth ski-line and neat holes where ski poles sank,
like stitches along an incision in the flesh of snow.

It took us 6 1/2 hours to travel the 6 1/2 miles to the Station,
Lincoln wrote, he and Paul Hansen climbing on skis,
up from Ephraim to this immense silence of mountains,
further stilled by snow. *We shoveled snow off roofs until dark.*
The moon reflected *like some vast pavement of angelic rhinestone.*

Next day they hiked on skis on up to Alpine, then skied
back down. Afterwards, worked to finish the snowy roofs.
On the East House it hung high & stubborn:
the day's triumph came when we cut it by sawing
the great pile with a manila rope and it avalanched
down at last burying us waist deep. The sensation
when you see the avalanche coming, is mingled fear
and pleasure—it swims about the body pleasantly.

Washing Windows

Ten new windows replacing
rippled old glass—frames long
painted shut—to open in summer,
trap heat in winter, all in need
of washing as Mother taught me,
vinegar and hot water, fumes
like pickling day, dried with a wad
of newspaper that turns to suede
on the third window, and then
a new clump. Nothing makes windows
shine better, clear as air. I wear
news of the day—children's
fathomless eyes as winter begins
in earthquake-ruptured Himalayas—
under my fingernails.

Long Johns

I wore them for skiing—a warm second skin,
buttoned up the front, the *barn door* buttoned

in back. Too warm when I dressed, just right
on slopes twenty feet deep in snow.

Coming off the hill, needing to pee, dancing
with urgency, I unlatched the cable of my skis,

stuck them in snow with the ski poles,
unmittened my freezing fingers, waited

my turn for the outhouse, then tried
to unbutton the barn door, legs pretzeled.

Washing

It took mother, wearing the pinafore
she'd made, more than a day each week
to keep us in clothes. Piles sorted, dark and light.
Electric agitator in the washtub, hand-made
brown soap, shaved, the hand-cranked wringer
squeezing water out of soaking sheets
hung out, matched up at corners so they'd
dry flat, socks paired and hung by toes
for easy rolling, shirts pinned along yoke seams,
dried in summer wind. It mattered
that neighbors kept an eye on her
housewifery. In winter, clothes hung
in the basement near the coal furnace
that made clinkers my father spread
on snowy sidewalks and we girls covered
in salt and water, a drop of bluing for a garden
of crystals. Everything hung up or neat in folded
piles, smelling of hot iron and mountain air.

Braided Rug

Patrick Healy pushed me in the mud
as I walked home from school for lunch,
dirtied my brand new beige tweed winter coat.

I worried: dry cleaning was expensive.
Whined about his torment. Mother asked,
What did you do to him? He was two grades

ahead, often kept me prisoned on a porch
I'd run to when he tried to bump me with his bike.
Mother said he must *like* me, but it seemed

to me he only liked to bully. When Grandma Eee
braided the rug now on my barn-red study floor,
she joined the stories of our winter coats.

Rock Island Line to Omaha, Union Pacific to Ogden
March 8, 1958

Mother's voice on the shared dormitory phone,
thinned by half a continent, *Daddy's gone. Come home.*

I bought train tickets for my sister and me
at the little station in Grinnell. As I rescheduled

mid-terms, one professor pressed a flask on me filled
with forbidden single-malt whiskey, *against shock.*

We tried it on the train in cone-shaped paper cups,
hardened our lips against its smoky slap.

For 36 hours we clanked and whistled across prairie,
antelope racing alongside, the train winding down

through Wyoming's startled rocks. Neighbors came
all day into night, bringing food, newspaper accounts

of the avalanche, the young rescuer also lost in snow,
his pregnant wife. Grandma Eee had keened, was now

dry-eyed and withered. We all shook hands, greeted
old friends, wreathed in condolences, found space

in the refrigerator for another jello salad, another pie
on the chilly back porch. We held up through the obsequies,

all of us on display. One woman told another who told us
we must not have cared much—we shed no tears.

After the funeral, Mother collapsed and I kneaded her back
till she slept, a rag doll whose stuffing had run out.

When crocuses, then daffodils came up through cold black soil
at the end of March, I called it resurrection. I poured the whiskey

in a Mason jar deep in my dorm closet, drank a glass
at graduation, poured the rest down the drain.

Mt. Ogden

From front window or porch, just beyond
the sycamore, close enough to touch,
nearly 10,000 feet of rocky splendor.

We skied on the backside, in Snow Basin,
hauled up School Hill by the modest
rope tow, a swaying chair lift up Wildcat.

Picnic tables and outdoor toilets
until the 2002 Winter Olympics brought
fancy lodges, higher lifts to take skiers

up into back country, where my father
hiked with climbers on his skis into
the massive silence of rock and snow.

In summer we hiked the side we faced,
towering above us every day in keen air.
When I went to college in Iowa I relished

prairie hills, smell of spring alfalfa,
fresh-turned earth. Back home—
how had I breathed all those months

without the sunrise leaking from behind
that west face of Mt. Ogden?—
days later, failed to notice.

Water Witch

In memory of Monroe Everett

He walked the land, hands holding a looping copper wire,
over fields and hills after spring rains. Their green
and wildflowers gave way to dun and amethyst. He

witched his own wells, wells for others in the valley,
brought water from the Colorado down to arid fields
and towns of southern California. Cal Tech-trained,

drawn throughout his life to the latest farm machinery,
flying farmer, he courted his second wife—my widowed
mother, the girl he'd fancied in high school—flying in,

bringing hothouse flowers, a diamond ring. She had never
been courted this way. With her he got four grown-up
daughters, then sons-in-law, eleven grandchildren.

He was my father longer than my father was.
A man of *bidness*, someone you could count on.
Blunt fingers scooped up the soil his crops grew in,

hefting earth from under orange trees. Three crops
at once: ripe fruit, green fruit and blossoms. Pollinating
bees made honey on Rattlesnake Hill behind the house.

He fingered earth from under avocados, walnuts,
oranges, where he, a young man, had first dry farmed.

What, someone asked him late in life, *was your most important
accomplishment?* He didn't miss a beat, said *Laurel and the girls.*

What She Lost Last

Mother held up a pair of baby blue
high-heeled shoes, gold embroidered,
the kind bridesmaids have dyed

to match a dress. She said, *Do you
think she'd like these?* I asked her, "Who?"
Well, you know, she answered, *Bob's wife.*

I said, *But I'm Bob's wife.* She puzzled.
Oh, yes, then brightened. *But do you think
she'd **like** them?* But at the piano she played

from her old Methodist hymnal as she, a girl,
had for her father's church. She could still
read aloud words on signs, the TV screen,

but didn't know what they meant. What
she lost last was her sociability:
she paid attention, smiled graciously.

Even when language had left, she held forth—
a generous, garbled kind of conversation,
a baby's babble girdled by grammar.

Inheritance

I'd like to drink a cup of coffee with my father
        at the kitchen table, red oak like satin under elbows,

cream colored mugs with wide blue bands, daffodils
        in the blue speckled jug, watching the backyard unwind

to green, trilliums blooming briefly while ferns push up
        their coiled fiddleheads and violets raise small faces.

We'd watch birds at the feeder and the squirrels that soar
        like arias in the ancient, damaged maple.

~

He wrote in his Montana journal, 1936, *to my astonishment*
        I found in the limestone a mass of sea shells! Seashells

4,000 ft. above Vigilante, itself 6,000 ft above the sea....
        what visionary mollusk ever dreamed that he would be lifted so high?

~

We'd laugh about the coffee sheepherders used to serve us
        from their wagons, along with mutton, sourdough biscuits,

tales of bears, coyotes, derring-do, coffee boiled, re-boiled, more grounds
        added 'til a spoon could stand alone.

~

I want to tell him all that's happened since that half a century ago
        on John Paul Jones Ridge, where he and three friends
equipped

with packs, first-aid supplies and tools rode the ski lift to the top,
        hiked, strips of moleskin strapped underside their skis,

the nap for traction, ate lunch, conversed among the trees.
        He led off, a downhill run, when the avalanche—silent

to one companion, a roar to the other—swept him down,
        buried him in fifteen feet of snow.

But if by magic we could share that cup of coffee, who would we be?
        He was six months shy of fifty when he died. I'm seventy-three.

~

He was slender, neat, his black brush cut, thick eyebrows,
        clear blue eyes looking out across mountains,

grieving irretrievable loss of soil, fingers showing me stamen
        and anther of a flower.

He read to us in the kitchen as we four did dinner dishes to keep us
        from fighting—Stevenson's *Black Arrow*,

the mysterious eye spying, from tapestry, up to no good,
        Lamb's *Essay on Roast Pig*, his delight in words.

He wrote his young wife, my mother, *Our language is a rich, beautiful one;*
        I love it, and do not like to see it mistreated.

Landslide on Rt. 65

We have learned that land mismanagement
may be followed closely by catastrophe.

Lincoln Ellison

The Pittsburgh Post Gazette said boulders
the size of refrigerators tumbled onto
Ohio River Boulevard, Rt. 65. Snapped
trees, utility poles, closed highway
and train tracks. The gas company shut
down its lines in case of rupture.
County, state, developer wrangled:
who should clear up the mess?

Plants had held the soil against gravity,
against the burrow of animals, rainfall,
snowmelt. This Allegheny County hill
was only a hill, but soil scraped off
for another Walmart was the miracle
of weathered rock, lichen, organisms,
plants that live, die, decay, enrich through
maybe a hundred thousand years or longer.

This little bit of land had survived the bite
of road and rail, this unremarkable hill.

Roundtrip

Lewis and Clark, sure they could reach the Pacific, came upon
ragged range after range, losing heart, hungry, cold. They

couldn't turn back. But I fly west over fields etched in winter's fallow
to snowy fabric rucked up into mountains, folded rocks laid down

by ancient seas, volcanic thrust and buckle. The engine vibrates
through the cold floor. From here snow looks dusted, though

it lies deep in those crevasses, on those peaks, nestled forests,
a range called Never No Summers. No telling if I'm seeing

rivers or valleys, what creatures hibernate, what germinates
in dark places, what soil enriches in decay. Now Cascades,

three volcanoes—Adams, Hood, Ranier—jagged surround
close enough to touch as the plane heads down through fog

to land. Earthbound, I take a bus downtown, eat mussels in sunshine
on Elliott Bay, edged by the snowy peaks I've just flown over.

Three days later I reverse: Cascades, desert, Great Salt Lake,
Wasatch Front, the badlands of Utah and Colorado flat and arid.

Coming in to Denver, foothills left behind, a rim of rose on the
        horizon
lights wispy clouds. We burn jet fuel and time coming in to land.

On east the sky blackens, lateness accelerates, one metropolis of lights
another, another, burning up the world I have just flown over.

Taking

When one tugs at a single thing in nature,
he finds it attached to the rest of the world.
John Muir

Great grandfather, Charles Thomas from mined-out Cornwall, joined
the Gold Rush, dug Grass Valley gold from underground, tailings
dumped downriver onto farmland. Miners dug up
12 billion tons of soil, injected mercury to flush out gold—
toxins in rivers, lakes, trees uprooted, floods. California natives

were in the way: infected with foreign pathogens, murdered—
100,000 killed, children taken from parents—just one of the costs
of get-rich-quick. By the time gold fever had died down,
streams and rivers were dammed, drained, poisoned.
Charles Thomas's grandson, my father, wrote how

overgrazing the Wasatch Plateau of south-central Utah
caused floods of mud and rock in valley towns. It had been
free for free-loading herders to run sheep and cattle along
the top, grazing between railheads, nipping off grasses and forbs
that held soil to steep slopes. Without vegetation to absorb

snow melt into hillsides, flooding followed Farmers, townsfolk
down in the valleys begged the Federal government for help.
Herders objected: if they couldn't use the land for free,
what was free-enterprise? Now gas companies want
what's under my city, my house, my back-yard garden

in which my daughter's ashes lie buried under Lenten roses.
Marcellus Shale, deep beneath us, full of natural gas that's been there
since before first mammals walked the earth. Wild-to-profit companies—
another Gold Rush, more herds free-grazing the Wasatch,
dollar signs worming greedy brains.

Rupturing Devonian rock, pouring chemicals in to force gas
up and out, rummaging in earth's great womb, flushing out
the time when forests and amphibians first appeared,
when fish became abundant, as the plates under everything
shift, capsize, collide.

Flick of a Bird

At the end of a marble hall in a sumptuous
art nouveau building—million dollar WPA project—

was my high school writing teacher's classroom.
Even the floors were marble. All Ogden used

the gilded auditorium: Utah Symphony, opera
where Don Jose had to stand on a box to stab

his willowy, doomed Carmen, *Rigoletto*'s Gilda
scaling vocal heights long after being stabbed

right where I was sure her lungs must be,
Paul Robeson's full-throated pain and glory.

When my daughter died I came to poetry again.
What delights me are the tiny poems—flick of a bird

quick across my retina—no plot, no argument.
Simply the moment, momentary, momentous.

Knuckle Bones

When Mother, about to marry again, cleaned out
our house, she gave me boxes of my father's papers:
his adolescent dairies—finding owl scat, observing bugs,
plans to backpack in San Gabriel Mountains
north-bordered by the San Andreas fault.

Almost daily journals, letters in his precise script,
drafts of articles. I got to know him long after
he died too young. Discovered his passion
for soil, eons in the making by wind, weather.

How vegetation held it to the mountain tops.
How Elk Knoll, hardly grazed, might be the closest thing
to primitive range, resistant to run-off. His delight
in the quilt of spruce, fir, aspen down toward Ephraim.
How marriage to my mother wasn't made in heaven,
how he'd hoped I'd be a son, how he chafed at bureaucrats.

Now, in the middle of the night when I can't sleep,
I ponder all our stuff to be sorted, thrown out, passed along.
Our old house, archaeological dig, potsherds, tenderly unearthed,
brushed off, matched up, past reconstructed out of knuckle bones.
Rich grain of tables and desks from my husband's workshop,
his table saw and planer. The marionettes I made—
witch with maroon yarn hair, grasping purple hands,
glittering iridescent eyes, king with jeweled crown,
paper maché face eaten away by mildew.

IV

My purpose, I think, is social: to lead people toward
sanity & wisdom by recovering the primitive environment.
To this end I can devote whatever aptitudes I have
in literary skill, scientific reasoning and love of the romantic.

—Lincoln Ellison, 1939

Aspen at Great Basis Experiment Station

Sue's Bones on Sioux Land

*The closest living relatives of the mighty predator
Tyrannosaurus rex are modern birds.*

New York Times, April 25, 2008

I look up from the newspaper into the old maple,
whose fallen blossoms green the walk below.

Who knew the dramas we've watched from here
were acted by aerial dinosaurs? Woodpeckers, routed

from nest and young by murdering starlings,
the blue jay that ripped apart the unfledged

cardinal baby. It was soft tissue in T-rex bones
matched up with birds', same protein passed link

to link down 68 million years. A complete T-Rex
named Sue stands in the Field Museum.

She's named for the woman who stayed behind
on Sioux land while her fellow archaeologists

took the flat tire into Faith, SD. Poking around
a cliff, she found her namesake, now reassembled,

13 feet high, 42 feet long, five-foot skull.
My son at four, asked, *Which came first, cowboys*

or dinosaurs? And now my grandson puzzles:
birds descendants of T-rex? *If you eat more*

you get smaller? It seems that we're evolved
from fish, brains encased in skulls, pairs of eyes,

ears, nostrils, arms, backbone, the brain's wiring,
sociable habits, hinged mouth and tongue,

matched rims of teeth. When the U.S. Government
in the nineteenth century defaulted on payments

to South Dakota Sioux, one white trader said,
they were *free to eat the grass.* The Sioux attacked

the trading post, murdered the trader, stuffed
his mouth with grass, 38 Sioux hanged.

Fighting followed: Dakota, Red Clouds,
Great Sioux wars, massacre at Wounded Knee.

T-Rex's teeth evolved to bite, rip, tear. Big fish
ate little fish, ventured out of water, onto land,

fins became fingers, made pots for soup, cooked meat.
Teeth got smaller: thus knives, guns and nukes.

I love the names of things

butterfly, bumblebee,
snowstorm, all airborne.

Worms turn the soil,
lavender stains my hands

with fragrance, lingering
in drawers and closets.

Columbine, pink and purple,
wild in my garden,

but in the Wasatch Mountains
a white so crystalline

it takes your breath. *Butter,*
churned and turned

into pats. *Cherries*
twinned by stems,

golden Queen Anne to ruby Bing,
from Persia to Rome.

When we picked them
from the long ladder,

we hung them in pairs
over our ears.

Pruning Roses in March

Today I began to prune the roses,
ragged canes above the slums
winter left behind, a wreckage—
soggy leaves, twigs, bits of paper,
the odd bottle cap, a mildewed
newspaper, still in its plastic jacket—
air fraught with granules of snow,
sky blue and wind like a paper cut,
getting in and round those hooks
of thorn to cut dead wood, dead canes,
those singed by winter cold.

Reading *Jane Eyre* On My Wedding Day in Inverness, California

A small wedding—$23 off-the-rack dress,
handmade veil. For the occasion, Bob's father

put sheets of Philippine mahogany on the walls
of the cabin, which glowed gold like honey.

We'd driven there the day before over muted hills
through redwoods' startling light and dark,

to the iridescence of Tomales Bay, air perfumed
with laurel—a landscape that was new to me.

My sister and I dressed the fireplace mantle with
camellias and hand-dipped candles from her wedding.

Then I was alone, a whole day to myself, reading
Jane Eyre and watching deer graze the hill below

among starry purple asters. I was just to the part
where Rochester's wife, kept captive as either mad

or driven mad in the attic, upends Jane's wedding
and it was time to wash my face, dress, comb my hair.

The groom, our parents, sisters and minister arrived.
Someone set Bach's unaccompanied cello suite playing

and I walked from the back bedroom to become
a wife in front of the blooming fireplace.

In 2010

the Texas Board of Public Education
tried to substitute *the Atlantic triangular trade*
for *the slave trade* in textbooks.

In Virginia the governor issued
a proclamation celebrating
the southern rebellion

against the United States—
it did not mention slavery.
When Republicans

elected to Congress in 2010
insisted on reading the Constitution
aloud on the floor of the House,

they deleted the part
that decreed a slave
should count as 3/5 of a person.

Naming

Mother and Daddy started it: *Laurel* and *Lincoln*.
Then *Liane*, named for the girl in a pencil drawing
given my mother by the first-grade child she taught.

The second child would be named for whichever parent,
so she was *Laurel*. Surely *Linda* would be a boy. But she
wasn't: her name, Spanish for *lovely*. Mother said

an 'ell of a family to shock the good people of Ephraim.
Then a miscarriage and another girl, *Linnea*,
for the mountain twinflower Daddy brought Mother

from his field trips. He read aloud to us, Lamb's "Essay
on Roast Pig," *Kidnapped*, *The Secret Garden*. We learned
to care for language as genetic code. Mother taught

the arts of housewifery—cooking, canning, sewing,
hanging laundry the right way. We grew up sturdy,
strong, knew not to complain. Both parents said

we *should take responsibility*, for each other, for the world.
In fifth grade I helped Daddy proofread his dissertation
for publication, *Subalpine Vegetation of the Wasatch Plateau*.

He read words and punctuation from the original:
I checked the galleys. Now in old age, my name haunts me
as *liana* vines strangle trees in tropical forests, rob them

of nutrients, climb, squeeze so the trees can't drink
the carbon humans pour into the air. Lianas pull water
out of soil, starve host trees. Enemies wearing my name.

Accidental Orchard

This morning when I took the compost out
to the fenced pile of leaves, kitchen waste
and fine, warm soil worked by worms,

there was an orchard of little avocado trees,
the large gold seeds split, stems standing
straight, thick with their exuberant foliage.

I marveled and pulled them out. They came
from the avocados my nephew grows
in southern California, orchards his grandfather—

my stepfather—planted. My nephew earns
his living designing posters for movie studios,
but also picks the avocados still hard—green

alligator skin—packs them in fine shredded
wood, sends them by mail to subscribers.
I let the avocados ripen indoors, feast all winter.

The Undressing

Like
a red
zipper
undoing
a green
dress
flaring
in wind
a cardinal
crosses
maple
leaves
riffling
light
framed
by my
window

So Good A Chair

Captain James D'Wolf commanded
the *Polly*, two-masted slaver. Feared
a sick slave had smallpox: the hold held
living merchandise.

He ordered sailors to tie her to a chair,
hoist her to the maintop. Left her
there two days, swaying out
over vast water. Twice light

gave way to darkness. Then
had her gagged, blindfolded, tossed
overboard. Some sailors refused.
She was of the Coromantee

seized on the Gold Coast, left
no name, how she was captured,
marched in a coffle to where she first saw
the *Polly* riding in harbor.

Then fetid stowage, fever, vomit.
To avoid indictment as abolition sentiment
ran high, D'Wolf sailed for Africa
while the case went before a grand jury.

A sailor, John Cranston, was brave to testify.
Asked *Do you recollect to hear the Captain say
any thing after the scene was ended?* he said,
He was sorry he had lost so good a Chair.

Found Amber

A beachcomber in southern England
found amber whose fossil resin

preserved for 140 million years
a whole spider, bits of web,

insect droppings, plant matter,
charred bark, burnt sap and microbes,

the earliest evidence of actinobacteria
that make soil by breaking down plants.

This eloquent amber! this whole museum!
The spider web was woven by the ancestor

of the common garden orb spider,
who launches her spokes of sticky silk

every evening, traps the traffic of night air
that strays into her free-hand geometry.

Each morning she wads up her web, eats it,
throws out new lines. She mates

as she needs to—sex with sixteen legs—
then often kills the hapless male.

Back Yard in Late Spring

This morning a yellow warbler lights the bird feeder,
a feathered flame. A baby starling—all claw,

stiletto beak—wrenches around, craning its neck,
too big to find a way in. A male cardinal, brilliant

even in this flowery spring, tries the same trick.
Purple finches line up on the nearest maple branch,

a pecking order for free and easy sunflower seeds,
while a squirrel tries to scramble from the nearby

window screen to launch himself around a corner
to the feeder. Making my daily survey of the cool

back yard, ferns, hostas, clematis and columbine,
I find the scrambled entrails of something small

glistening on the path, a ruby globule, trail of frayed
intestine, wash it under a fern for ants to dispose of.

Surely there's larger meaning here in this back yard
a-swarm with life, with death. But maybe none

beyond this: that this little world is the world.

Paper Dolls

The summer I went through all my stuff,
    the summer after Mother re-married and I
        had either to throw out childhood, or take it along,

I disposed of my marionette stage with gold
    proscenium, red velvet curtains and footlights
        that dimmed and sharpened with a rheostat.

And the big flat box of paper dolls I'd made
    through summers at the Alpine Cabin, above
        timber, those black nights indoors

by kerosene lantern with its glowing
    mantle and the insects that pestered its chimney.
        There were all the characters of fairy tales,

the Oz books, *Alice in Wonderland*, drawn on
    the backsides of used paper, colored
        with Prang paints and Crayolas, cut out

with Mother's scissors and stored in the big
    candy box that once held chocolates
        in ruffled cups.

Mother's Cookie Sheet

Old crusted, rusted sheet
for biscuits, cookies, pizza crusts,

roasted vegetables, coated with
burned-on drips and drippings,

on edge with my newer 40-year-oold
cookie sheets and roasting pans

in the upright cupboard, Chinese
red paint, chipped and bruised

where all these pans have been
slid out and in over and over.

If Stars

If the stars
we see at night

aren't there....
if what we see

are mere echoes
of ancient light,

their source
having retreated,

burned out....
if what we

write sonnets to
is the memory

of light,
its fading

reputation,
by which

we've pledged
undying love,

caught breath
at its brilliance....

Lightning

Air thick as cotton batting. Rain
drives down gray air like pounded nails.
Drumming water beats a tattoo

on the roof, on maple leaves.
Crack! like gunshot. The clock
explodes off the wall, knocks

a picture to the barn-red floor.
Searing along my right arm and leg,
a singe tingles inside my skin for hours.

Lightning's left its burn before
on our big Norway maple,
on a smaller volunteer;

once zapped everything electronic
and hurled the girl next door
across her front hall floor.

Four million bolts a day from six miles up.
It may be they're set off when sparks
from electrons spill from dying stars.

That shocking scorch pulsed along my arm,
deep in my hip, rearranged the atoms
in my bloodstream.

Falling

Crossing the frigid bridge over
the Mississippi in Minneapolis
to get to nursery school in winter,

I couldn't move, not forward,
not back, naked in the rush
of people on foot, in cars, in buses,

then I'm on the dirt road gouged
out of the mountainside on the right,
sheer drop on the left, while

a grizzly bears down, moving
massively, edging me, my naked feet
testing the crumble of loose dirt.

In second grade a girl said that if
you hit bottom in a dream you die.
I wanted then to wake, plummeting,

full of consternation, but now I fall
leisurely, turning over and over,
floating, a downward dance

alongside my beloved. We're falling
together, towards one another,
as our bones thin and brittle.

Tree

Today they are cutting down
the old maple in the backyard,

a crew of three men, one
on a machine with long neck

that raises him into high branches;
one who has dismantled a part

of the fence that hugs the tree;
one wearing spikes, his chain saw

and other tools hooked to his belt;
high up, cutting thick branches

among dense leaves, working back
towards the scarred and damaged trunk.

The old maple has blushed faint
green in spring, glowed gold in fall,

spun lace in winter, runway and airport
for squirrels, birds—an owl one year—

a pair of woodpeckers who nested,
laid eggs: a starling killed the chicks.

But it's older than we are old
and might come crashing down.

It's being dismantled, the way
age dismantles, higher branches

cut first, then pruned back
until we can see from the sliced

raw trunk—twelve feet around—
an account of age. At dinner time,

three squirrels, tentative, peer
over the fresh stump,

perplexed that their whole world
has vanished.

Notes

Lincoln Ellison's papers—journals, letters and publications—are archived at Utah State University Library, Logan, UT.

The Great Basin Experiment Station, which has existed under several names, was created as a Forest Service research facility in 1912. Wendell Keck's history of the Station explains the torrent of requests to the Secretary of Agriculture "for scientific study of summertime floods that originated on mountain watersheds and were seriously damaging farms and rural communities in the West. Such floods, of mud and rocks, were especially severe and frequent in valley communities below the Wasatch Plateau...." *Great Basin Station: Sixty Years of Progress in Range and Watershed Research*, USDA Forest Service Research Paper INT-118, 1972, Intermountain Forest and Range Experiment Stations, Ogden, Utah 84401.

The Alpine Cabin, at just under 11,000 feet, is an old snow surveyor's cabin owned by the Forest Service. Two water-collection sheds on the adjoining steep slopes have helped researchers measure run-off under various grazing conditions.

A few persons from the Station are mentioned. Nathalie Hansen was the daughter of Ruth and Paul Hansen, the Station's foreman, jack-of-all-trades, storyteller and handyman. Nathalie was my first best friend. Mama Dell was the cook at the Lodge, where visiting scientists and other guests stayed.

p. 12 "Rain Shadow" Just as an ordinary shadow is the area on which the sun, blocked by some object, does not fall, a rain shadow is the dry area cast on the lee side of a mountain on which the moisture that precipitates on the windward side does not fall.

p. 13 "Fathom" A fathom is 1.83 meters or six feet. 234 fathoms is 1,400 feet.

p. 18 "Waiting," The CCC was the Civilian Conservations Corps, organized under ECW, or Emergency Conservation Work legislation, during the Great Depression to alleviate unemployment and restore the country's natural resources through public works, 1933.

p. 21   "Great Basin Experiment Station," "[W]ith the starlight on our faces" is a quotation from Rudyard Kipling, "The Feet of Young Men," *The Five Nations*.
The final quotation is from Marcus Hall, "Repairing Mountains: Restoration, Ecology, and Wilderness in Twentieth-Century Utah," *Environmental History*, VI #4, October 2001, p. 595.

p. 27   "Mother Sewing," mentions the requirement to "take a formal" to college. Not so clear now, it was perfectly clear at the time: a formal was a fancy—often long—gown for formal dances, for which one had to have a "date."

p. 34   "Cemetery," Elk Knoll is not far from the Alpine Cabin above Ephraim, Utah. ATV refers to All Terrain Vehicle; ORV refers to Off Road Vehicle.

p. 40   "On Top," Quadrats are fenced meter-square experimental plots. At the time Lincoln Ellison wrote his dissertation, *Subalpine Vegetation of the Wasatch Plateau, Utah,* he was charting and photographing 52 quadrats, most of which had been established in the early 1900's. Since these quadrats were protected against grazing by large wild or domestic animals, they provided some measure of the damage done by grazing and the capacity of ungrazed rangeland to recover its vegetation.

p. 82   "So Good a Chair," is based on a story in Marcus Rediker's splendid book, *The Slave Ship*, Penguin Books, 2008.

Liane Ellison Norman was born in the Rocky Mountains of Montana, the eldest of four daughters of a Forest Service range ecologist and an elementary school teacher. She grew up in the Wasatch Mountains of Utah, was educated in Iowa and Massachusetts, gave birth to the middle of three children in Kathmandu, Nepal and has lived in Pittsburgh, PA for the last 45 years. She has been a writer all her life: in the fifth grade she wrote her biography-and bound stitched-together pages in fabric-covered boards with pasted-down end pages.

Norman won the Wisteria Prize for poetry in 2006 from Paper Journey Press. She has published two earlier books of poetry, *The Duration of Grief* and *Keep*, a book about nonviolent protest against nuclear bomb parts makers, *Mere Citizens: United, Civil and Disobedient*, a biography, *Hammer of Justice: Molly Rush and the Plowshares Eight*, and *Stitches in Air: A Novel About Mozart's Mother*. Two recent chapbooks of her poetry are *Roundtrip* (Yesterdays Parties Press) and *Driving Near the Old Federal Arsenal* (Finishing Line Press.)

CPSIA information can be obtained at www.ICGtesting.com
Printed in the USA
BVOW011505160912

300465BV00002B/1/P

9 781933 964614